Rise of the Zombie Scarecrows

Deb Loughead

Orca currents

ORCA BOOK PUBLISHERS

Library and Archives Canada Cataloguing in Publication

Loughead, Deb, 1955–, author
Rise of the zombie scarecrows / Deb Loughead.
(Orca currents)

Issued in print and electronic formats.
ISBN 978-1-4598-0996-3 (pbk.)—
ISBN 978-1-4598-0998-7 (pdf).—ISBN 978-1-4598-0999-4 (epub)

I. Title. II. Series: Orca currents
PS8573.O8633R58 2015   jc813'.54   c2014-906683-x
c2014-906684-8

First published in the United States, 2015
Library of Congress Control Number: 2014952066

Summary: Fifteen-year-old Dylan is making a short film about zombie scarecrows,
but Halloween pranksters are making his progress difficult.

*Orca Book Publishers is dedicated to preserving the environment and has
printed this book on Forest Stewardship Council® certified paper.*

Orca Book Publishers gratefully acknowledges the support for its
publishing programs provided by the following agencies: the Government
of Canada through the Canada Book Fund and the Canada Council for the Arts,
and the Province of British Columbia through the BC Arts Council
and the Book Publishing Tax Credit.

Cover photography by Getty Images
Author photo by Steve Loughead

ORCA BOOK PUBLISHERS
PO Box 5626, Stn. B
Victoria, BC Canada
V8R 6S4

ORCA BOOK PUBLISHERS
PO Box 468
Custer, WA USA
98240-0468

www.orcabook.com
Printed and bound in Canada.

18 17 16 15 • 4 3 2 1

For Ben and Star,
"happy creators" who always inspire.

Chapter One

"Aren't you too old for trick-or-treating, Dylan?" Gran put down her knitting and stared at me from her usual spot on the saggy sofa.

Gran was great at sticking it to me.

"We're not 'trick-or-treating,' Gran." I even used air quotes. "It's a project for our media class. We need to make a short film, and ours has a Halloween theme.

So we're wearing costumes while we film on Halloween night."

"Hmm, sounds like a *good excuse* to me." She clicked her tongue and her knitting needles at the same time.

Wow, sticking it to me *twice* in one minute. That had to be a new record.

"Honestly, it's not an excuse, Gran," my friend Cory told her. All my friends called her Gran. She pretty much insisted on it. "It's an important project."

"We've worked hard planning this for almost all of October," Monica added. "It counts for 50 percent of our grades this semester."

Which was the *undead* truth.

"Hmm. Is that so?" Gran squinted at us.

"Honestly, Gran, everything's cool," I reassured her. "And trust me, you will get a huge kick out of this movie. I wish I could tell you more, but it's top secret."

Gran raised her eyebrows. "I see," she said. "Now I'm *very* curious. But you know I trust you to do the right thing."

She was so good at laying guilt trips on me.

Cory stared at me, wide-eyed, sending a silent message to keep my mouth shut. Yup, it was probably best not to mention that we were making a zombie flick. I'd been obsessed with them ever since I saw *World War Z* and read the book. Then there was *Zombieland* and *Warm Bodies*. *Shaun of the Dead* and *The Walking Dead*. The whole *undead* explanation probably wouldn't go over very well with Gran, though, even if she knew what a zombie was.

It wasn't easy to keep my mouth shut about our movie. We were totally pumped because we'd figured out a brand-new spin on the zombie thing. During the month of October in Bridgewood, a scarecrow contest takes over the whole town. Nearly every property has at least one scarecrow on display. Even shop owners on the main drag participate. On November 1, All Hallows Day, judges from the Chamber of Commerce wander around to check out all the displays. Prizes are awarded for "most original," "most terrifying" and "most adorable." So we figured a movie about *zombie* scarecrows would be the coolest ever! In keeping with the spirit of the town, of course. Not much difference between scarecrows and zombies anyway, apart from straw and rotting flesh.

Gran's mouth had turned into a tight knot. When Monica noticed, she snuggled up beside Gran on the sofa. Ever since the summer, when Monica and I had become closer after helping the police solve a local break-and-enter crime, Gran had been crazy about her. All Monica had to do was give her that brilliant smile, and Gran would melt.

"Aw, Gran," she said. "We know grade ten is too old to go out for Halloween. This is our way of taking part. Who are you knitting those socks for? They're so pretty—all those blue and green and purple shades."

"I know you're sweet-talking me, Monica," Gran said. "I'm knitting these socks for you. I hope you like the color."

"Wow! Cool! I love them, thanks."

"And I know I won't have to worry if you're going to keep an eye on things. Dylan has a bad habit of—"

"Getting up to no good," I said, finishing her favorite sentence. "And technically, none of it has ever been my fault."

"That's what Nicole always tries to tell me," Gran said, and I winced. Nicole Vance, a local police officer, was also my mom's best friend. They'd grown up together in our town. Somehow Nicole was always involved in my little adventures.

Deb Loughead

"You're the best, Gran," Monica said and gave her arm a squeeze. It was a good distraction from talking about Nicole, but she meant it too. Monica had to be the most honest person I'd ever known.

She was also a really good kisser, I'd discovered over the summer. "I'm so glad you're watching *It's the Great Pumpkin, Charlie Brown* with the three of us tonight," she said.

Gran leveled her gaze at us. "*Technically*, I'm letting you fellas watch *Charlie Brown* with *me* tonight." Then she gave us one of her trademark winks.

Ah, that Gran of mine. She was great at sticking it to all of us.

On the Monday before Halloween, we put up the zombie casting-call posters in the hallways at school. We weren't the only ones feeling bad about being too old for trick-or-treating. Until you're fourteen, you can sort of get away with it. Especially if you haven't had a huge growth spurt yet. I was still waiting for mine.

But by the time you're nearly *sixteen*, and I'd be turning sixteen in November, going door-to-door with all the little kids is pretty lame. Besides, big kids showing up at the door freaks out most candy donors. Sometimes they yell at you and shut the door in your face. That happened to us last year.

"Wow, Monica, you rock at art," I told my girlfriend. Yes, *girlfriend*. "Those zombies look just like a real movie poster."

She gave me that killer smile. "It's my passion, Dylan. Like you wanting to be a filmmaker someday. We're both kind of crazy and artsy." She brushed her hand across mine, and as usual I melted from the inside out.

"Let's hope some kids show up for the casting call on Wednesday," Cory said. "Who wouldn't want to dress up like a zombie scarecrow for Halloween night and scare all the little kids?"

"*Rise of the Zombie Scarecrows*," I growled, grinning. "Personally, I think it's a totally brilliant title."

"You would," Cory said. He stepped aside when a group of students crowded in front of the poster to admire Monica's artwork.

"I sure hope some of the older kids from Theater Arts and the drama club come and audition," Monica said.

"Oh, they will," I told her. "They've got a long wait till the spring drama production."

"This sounds totally cool," one of the guys said. I recognized him, a senior named Henry. He was in the drama club last year and had played a lead role in a production of *Guys and Dolls*. He was

8

tall and thin. I already had him pegged for the part of the main zombie.

"You need girls, too, right?" said Helena, the girl who was with him. She'd had a starring role in the play last year too.

"Of course," Monica told her. "There are girl zombies in every flick. Come and audition. And bring your friends too."

"Nice artwork, Monica," Helena said. "For sure we'll be there Wednesday."

As they walked away, I gave Monica a high five. "Wow. She actually knows my name," Monica whispered, sounding starstruck.

"Cool. Henry and Helena," I said. "That's *exactly* who I was hoping for."

Then someone bumped into me hard from behind. I spun around. *Oh great.* Garrett, standing there with his goofy grin. This guy had been giving me grief for a few years now. Our friendship was on and off. Most of the time he was a huge nimrod.

"Wow, did your girlfriend draw this?" he said, eyeing Monica. I think he was jealous that I was dating someone as awesome as her.

"I'm standing right here," Monica said. "And yes, I drew *all* the posters we put up around the school."

"So what's the buzz? You're making a zombie movie? Can anyone be in it?"

Uh-oh. He was the *last* person on earth I wanted to audition. Whenever he and his buddies turned up, something was sure to go wrong.

"Yeah, well, we're kind of looking for drama students to take roles," I explained in as nice a way as I could manage.

"Huh. So you don't want football players and non-advanced-stream kids then. Right? That's kind of racist, isn't it?"

Monica rolled her eyes and Cory grimaced. I just sighed.

"Not exactly," I told him. "We just want to give the drama kids a chance to be in something this fall. *Okay*?"

"Maybe. Maybe not. *Auditions in the auditorium after school Wednesday*," he read from the poster. "Cool. See ya then, dudes. And dudette."

As he stomped away, I had a fleeting thought that he'd make a good zombie. But I stomped that thought out as Monica stood there shaking her head.

"Dud*ette*? Seriously?" she said. "God, Dylan, I sure hope he *doesn't* show up for this."

Funny, I half hoped he would. I'd *never* admit that to Monica though!

Chapter Two

Every October as far back as I can remember, the town of Bridgewood has taken on a surreal atmosphere. It almost literally becomes a ghost town. But in a good way.

It's my favorite time of year. The invasion of the "cidiot" cottage dwellers has basically ended, but we haven't been buried in snow yet. The whole town seems to glow gold and orange because of the turning leaves. That brings in busloads of tourists, but at least it's a short season.

The best part of October leading up to Halloween is the scarecrow competition. Nearly every home on every street is set up like a haunted house or a crime scene. Especially the homes that have kids my age living in them. Is there anything better than creating a blood-spattered gore fest on your front lawn?

Even we apartment dwellers get in on the fun. During October there are always a couple of dead bodies slumped over our balcony or dangling from a noose to scare anyone who dares to look up. One year, Gran caught me as I was about to drip ketchup on them. Another year I dropped one of the "bodies" from a rope a couple of times. I stopped after a little kid started screaming blue murder when it landed in front of her. It didn't go over very well.

This year, our balcony scarecrows were dead athletes with half-deflated basketballs for heads. Cory and I attached grotesque rotting-face masks made out of rubber. They made Mom shiver for real. Gran was sure she'd be having nightmares.

I brought Monica home for dinner with Gran and me after school. Mom was working an evening shift at Rocky's Roadhouse, where she was bar manager. Lots of guys liked to drop by there for a pint or two and some spicy wings. And to talk to my mom as she worked the bar. I'd seen them flirting with her often, but they were wasting their time. My mom had handed her heart to a guy named Brent, who came up from the city most weekends. Not a typical cidiot, he was self-employed and thinking of relocating here to be closer to her. I figured it would be weird to have some-thing like a dad if that ever happened.

Gran served us her made-from-scratch mac and cheese with cut-up weiners. Then Monica and I worked on homework until nearly seven thirty. It felt great sitting right beside her at the kitchen table, our shoulders touching as she helped me out with math, which I suck at. But right between *Wheel of Fortune* and *Jeopardy!*, Gran had to ruin it.

"Time for you to be getting ready for bed soon, Dylan," she said. "You'd better take Monica home now."

"God, Gran," I said and groaned. "I'm not five years old anymore."

"Still," she said. "You have to cross town, so get moving. Your mom expects it."

"Mom doesn't care what time I go to bed," I reminded my grandmother, "as long as I'm in my room by ten. Which gives me two and a half hours to get Monica home."

"Nice seeing you tonight, Monica," Gran called over her shoulder. "Come on over anytime. Hurry back, please, Dylan. Don't make me worry about you."

"Jeez, Gran!" I yelped. Yet another guilt trip to drive me nuts.

"It's okay, Dylan," Monica said close to my ear, and she put her hand over mine. Instant warm rush. "I've got to get going anyway. Mom wants me home by eight."

I helped her gather her stuff, and then we thumped down the echoing apartment stairway. Out on the dim and windy street, the rattle of dry leaves sounded a bit like scarecrow foot-steps. Monica kept glancing over her shoulder, and then she snuggled in closer, so I wrapped my arm around her. She slipped hers around my waist.

We stopped to kiss in the shadows more than a few times as we crossed town. We also stopped to admire the scarecrows arranged in eerie scenes in front yards and in shop windows on every street. And the jack-o'-lanterns that were lit up in so many windows already.

"This Halloween is gonna be the best ever," I said as we walked along. "The film is a no-brainer to shoot. I wish I had the ending figured out though."

"Yeah, that is kind of important," Monica said. "You know, I was thinking maybe we should tell Officer Vance before we do any filming. In case there's, like, an…an incident or something."

I stopped dead under a streetlight, put my hands on Monica's shoulders and looked right into her delicious chocolate-brownie eyes.

"Can't happen," I told her. "Because you already know how that will go. Right?"

Monica sighed. "She probably won't approve. I just hope you don't make the news for the third time in a year," she murmured. "I mean, that would be—"

I planted a long soft kiss on her lips before she could finish her sentence. It was a good one, too, because I heard her sigh again. Our lips froze in that position, though, when we heard yells and running footsteps not far off. Monica yanked herself away, grabbed my arm and pulled me behind a gigantic tree trunk.

"Look," she said, pointing down the gloomy street.

In the pools of light from the street lamps, we could see something running fast. It was headed straight in our direction. I heard Monica start to breathe harder as we both realized what we were seeing. Not far behind it, an old man seemed to be chasing it down.

"What *is* that creepy thing?" she said. "What's going on here?"

"*Crap*! Am I *really* seeing a scarecrow? Running down the street?" I said.

When it passed only a few feet away from us, I sucked in my breath. It had a hideous face.

"*Zombie* scarecrow?" I hissed.

Beside me, Monica's whole body was trembling. "Let's get out of here *fast*."

But we couldn't. Because right that second, the old man fell over. He collapsed in a heap right there in the middle of the road.

"*Crap*!" I yelled again, and we both ran over to him.

Monica crouched and started shaking his shoulders. He looked scary —pale and half dead. My arms and legs turned all rubbery.

"Sir? *Sir*? Can you hear me, sir?" she kept saying.

"Is he *dying*? Please don't let him be dying," I murmured.

Monica reached into her pocket and shoved her cell phone at me.

"Call 9-1-1," she said. Then she started pumping on the center of the man's chest with both hands. And singing some oldies song, "Stayin' Alive," over and over again.

My fingers kept hitting the wrong numbers on her phone. "You're supposed to breathe into his mouth, aren't you, Monica?" I said. "And what's with the song?"

"Just call the number, Dylan!"

This time I got it right and told them to come quick. Monica kept pumping on the man's sternum. She looked like a crazy girl, her face taut, dark eyes gleaming in the orange glow of the street-lights. Willing the old man to stay alive.

I couldn't even move, I was so scared. And underneath it all, I felt ashamed for not having a clue what I was supposed to be doing. For not leaping into action like Monica had. I just knelt on the road beside her and made gentle circles on her back until I heard the sirens.

The first person to zoom up to the scene was Officer Nicole Vance. Thank God the ambulance was right on her tail. Before Nicole could get out of the cruiser, I leaned closer to Monica and touched the top of her head.

"Let me do the talking, okay?" I told her. She nodded hard as the EMTs swarmed around us and efficiently took over her job.

Nicole and I helped Monica to her feet. She was still trembling.

"Are you okay?" I asked, as a couple of rivulets of mascara trickled down her cheeks. She brushed them away, nodded and tried to smile, then burst into tears.

"So Mr. Dalton was just hurrying along the street and he collapsed?" Nicole asked.

Mr. Buddy Dalton. The grandpa of a grade-nine kid I knew. Timothy, with the 007 actor's name. In the rearview mirror, I caught a glimpse of Nicole's eyes watching mine as she drove us home. When I felt Monica squirming beside me in the backseat, I squeezed her hand.

"We were kind of hiding behind a tree, you know. And we were, like…"

"I *get* it," Nicole said. "Making out. So then what? What did you see? Or hear?"

"So we didn't see much. Just heard shouts and footsteps and saw him fall."

"Like he was chasing someone or something?" Nicole asked.

Monica stiffened, and I squeezed her hand harder. "Yeah, like that, I guess."

"I sure hope he makes it," Nicole murmured. "He used to run the candy store. Years ago when your mom and I were kids. Nutty Buddy, we called him. After those ice-cream cones."

I gulped. Monica's hand went limp in mine. When we pulled up to her house, her mom was waiting in the doorway. I hoped Monica wouldn't tell her what had happened. If anyone found out we'd seen a zombie scarecrow running down the street, our epic movie would be toast.

"Thanks, Officer Vance," Monica said when Nicole let her out of the car. "Don't worry, I'll explain everything to my mom. You can just take Dylan home now."

Then she slammed the car door. Without even saying goodbye to me.

Chapter Three

I got lucky that night in one way. Nicole let me off in front of the apartment and didn't even come up to blab anything to Gran. So I just said goodnight when I passed her on the sofa watching *Doc Martin* and went straight to bed. I tried to fall asleep without fixating on what had happened in the car with Monica.

It worked, too, until someone started shaking me at eleven thirty. When I opened my eyes, the light was on in my room. And three faces were staring down at me. Gran and Mom. And Nicole.

"Mr. Dalton is okay, Dylan," she said. "In fact, I was just talking to him a while ago at the hospital. It was a mild heart attack. But he's a tough old guy. He'll be fine."

"Well, that's great then. Thanks for letting me know. Hi, Gran. You're home early, Mom. Goodnight, everyone." I pulled the covers over my head. Instantly they were yanked back off.

"Mr. Dalton told Nicole he was chasing a scarecrow down the street," Mom told me.

Gran stood there frowning and clucking her tongue in a knowing way.

"What does that have to do with the price of eggs?" I said. And probably shouldn't have.

Gran clucked her tongue even louder. I hoped she wouldn't say it.

"Well, obviously *someone* was up to no good," she muttered. Yeah, I guess it was too much to hope for after all.

I sat up in bed. I looked them all straight in the eye, one by one.

"Is it not enough that we saved the old guy's life?" I said. "And now you think it was *our* fault that he collapsed?"

"I never said that," Nicole told me. "I just want to know what you saw. By the way, I believe it was Monica who performed CPR on him. Apparently, she's taken a lifesaving course. Cool, huh?"

I swallowed hard. "How do you even know all this?" I asked.

Thick silence. That wasn't a good sign.

"I went back to Monica's place after I dropped you off. To interview her alone," Nicole said. "She told me what you saw. And also said you didn't want to tell me. How come?"

I felt something wither inside me. I couldn't even look at them anymore.

"*Why*, Dylan?" Mom whispered, then sat down on the edge of my bed. An even worse sign. "What's going on with you?"

"Nothing," I said. "*Nothing* is going on with me."

"You're not dealing drugs, are you?" Gran said. "Because if he is, Stephanie, then—"

"Mom, cool it, okay?" my mom said to her. "I'm sure it's nothing to do with drugs." A long pause. "Am I *right*, Dylan?" Her eyes pleaded for reassurance.

"God, of course not," I said. "Because if I was, then for sure Officer Vance would have caught me by now! Am I right, Nicole?"

At least that made them all smile for a few seconds.

"Look. I also heard about that movie you're making," Nicole added, and I

27

sucked in my breath. "About zombie scarecrows on Halloween night. It's not a good idea."

"See? I knew you'd want to shut this whole thing down if you found out. *That's* why I didn't want Monica to blab about what we saw tonight."

I tightened my jaw, bit down on the inside of my cheek and tried my best not to start crying. Because the truth was, I was starting to feel like total crap about this whole thing. Monica looked like some sort of CPR-performing superhero, and I looked like a superloser.

"Don't flatter yourself, Dylan. Because this isn't about you," Nicole told me, straight up like usual. "This isn't about your film project or about Monica or even poor old Mr. Dalton, who is going to be fine, thank God. It's actually about the scarecrow."

"The scarecrow?" the rest of us said in unison.

"Okay, we're not going to broadcast this because we want to avoid copycats," Nicole told us. "But over the weekend there was another weird incident like this one on the same street. Started with a knock on someone's front door after dark. When the homeowner opened it, a really freaky-looking scarecrow was standing there, holding a lit jack-o'-lantern."

"Oh gosh," Gran said. "That would scare the living daylights out of me."

"I know, and it gets worse," Nicole said. "Because as soon as the homeowner opened the door, the scarecrow pitched the pumpkin into the house, then ran away laughing like a maniac."

"Oh my god," Mom said. "That's ridiculous."

"And dangerous," Gran added. "That could start a fire!"

"And who the he...*eck* is doing it, Nicole?" I said, catching myself.

"Language, please, Dylan," Gran said, squinting.

"We don't know. But we sure want to find out. Mr. Dalton heard about the first incident from his neighbor. That's why he chased the scarecrow this time. He hates the thought of not feeling safe in his own home."

My mouth was hanging open. "Wow, that is *insane*," I said. "I wonder who—"

"Stay out of this, Dylan," Nicole and Mom said in one voice. And Gran clucked.

"A gem of a man, that Buddy Dalton," she said.

"Oh *god*. All *right* already," I said. "You don't all have to go ballistic on me!"

"But you can clearly see the problem with making that movie on Halloween this Saturday, right?" Nicole said, and I winced. "I mean, we can't have a bunch of random scarecrows running around town when we're trying to find real troublemakers."

"O*kaaay*," I said. "But my whole film project is *based* on Halloween night. And it's due a week later. So that means I won't have a film to turn in on time for my media class."

"You're a smart guy. I'm sure you'll think of something," Nicole said. "And I'm sure your teacher will understand if you explain. Please. This can't happen, and you know it."

I gritted my teeth, nodded and tried to smile. "Okay, so good night," I said.

This time when I pulled the covers over my head, nobody pulled them off.

I hardly slept the rest of that night. I tossed and turned and got mummified by my covers. Sometime during the night I got up to eat a bowl of Cheerios, and I watched a lame old Frankenstein movie for a while. Back in bed, I started counting sheep, then scarecrows, and that didn't help.

It wasn't because I was worried about the scarecrow vandal and his pumpkin bomb. Or the zombie movie I had to figure out a way to make and the script that wasn't quite finished. Or poor old Mr. Dalton. Or how Nicole was probably going to be on me like a duck on a June bug, as Gran liked to say.

Nope, none of that. I couldn't sleep because I couldn't stop thinking about Monica.

"You figure she's avoiding you because she's mad?" Cory asked me in the cafeteria at lunch on Tuesday. I had just finished filling him in on what had happened the night before. I told him all about the scarecrow vandal after he promised to keep his mouth shut. I even confessed how stupid I felt that Monica was the only one who could help save Mr. Dalton's life. Of course, everyone had clapped for her, in every classroom, after the principal announced the news on the PA system.

"Guess so. She hasn't even *looked* at me today. She walked right past me on the school bus this morning, and we *always* sit together. And she ignored me when I said hi in the hallway."

"So maybe she's got a bunch of other stuff on her mind," Cory said.

"Thanks. *Not* helpful," I said, then bit into the tuna-salad sandwich Gran had fixed me that morning. She'd skimped on the mayo, and no chopped-up apples either. Which meant she was probably still mad about last night too. "So what should I do?"

"Dude, seriously, I know nothing about girls," Cory confessed. He sighed. "I've never even kissed a girl. And if you tell *anyone* that, I'll have to kill you."

He grinned and nudged me with his elbow. "Anyway, I'm sure she'll get over it. Eventually."

I kept glancing across the cafeteria toward the table where Monica was sitting. If it was over with her and me, well, I guess I was lucky I'd had the chance to be her boyfriend for a while.

Monica was sitting with Charlie Wells, a senior most girls crushed on. Just like back in middle school, when he'd started breaking hearts. He was in Theater Arts too. And Monica liked artsy types.

"Quit staring at her," Cory said. "You look freakin' desperate."

"Whatever. Want the rest of my tuna-salad sandwich?"

It was in his hand before I could blink.

"So what about our movie then?" he said through a mouthful. "We're screwed now, right? And Monica is in our group. What's *she* gonna do? Join another group?"

"Stop asking me questions I can't answer," I told him. "When I think of something, you'll be the first to know. Because this movie still has to happen. There's no time to pull anything else together."

"Okay," Cory said. "Are those home-made gingersnap cookies? Are you gonna eat them?"

I pushed the cookies across the table and glanced over at Monica again. For an instant she looked right back at me. But she wasn't even close to smiling. And she looked away as soon as her eyes met mine. Her chocolate-brownie eyes.

I missed those eyes already.

Monica avoided me the entire day. When I tried to talk to her in class a few times, she just ignored me. When we passed in the hall, she made a point of keeping her head down. And after school, there was a note jammed in the crack of my locker when I went to open it.

Dylan, I need this mark. I can't risk it. So I'm helping Ivy and Sasha shoot their movie Wednesday night. And editing it over the weekend. Sorry it didn't work out with your movie. Good luck. M.B.

Great. So it really was over. I stared at the inside of my locker for about five minutes, feeling like an undead under my skin. Until I realized Cory was beside me.

"Bad news?" he said. When he pointed at the note in my hand, I passed it to him.

"Ivy *Adams*? Hmm," he murmured. I knew for a fact that he was crushing on Ivy big-time. "So Monica's done with us then?"

"Pretty much." I stuffed the note in my back pocket. "Looks like it's just you and me."

"So how do we pull this off without getting Officer Vance mad at us? What's the plan?"

I looked him in the eye. "The plan isn't changing. It's just…shifting. I have an idea. But you can't tell a single living human being. Got it?"

We walked home together instead of taking the bus, so I wouldn't have to face Monica. As we walked, I told him my plan. That was the one good thing that had come from being alone with my dismal thoughts most of the day instead of focused on Monica's sweet face. I mostly daydreamed about how to make our movie happen anyway, even after Nicole's warning. Cory listened wide-eyed, looking extremely doubtful.

"Look, Cory," I told him. "If things work out the way I've planned tomorrow night, we'll actually be doing the Bridgewood police department a huge favor. Am I right, or what?"

Cory gulped hard. "I sure hope so," he said. "And I sure hope Officer Vance agrees with you. And *doesn't* decide to arrest us."

When I got to the apartment, Gran was all perky and asked if my lunch was okay. I just shrugged. Then she asked how Monica was. So I shrugged again and walked straight to my room. Which is exactly where I stayed for the rest of the night. I tried to work on the script for a while, but I felt totally brain dead. And my heart kind of hurt too.

At one point I found the courage to call Monica. It took me three tries to dial her number with jittery fingers. When the phone rang, her mom answered. She said Monica was busy and couldn't talk to me right then.

I was actually blinking back tears when I hung up.

"Looks like Monica made the papers this time," Gran told me as soon as I walked into the kitchen the next morning. Mom was sitting at the table, still disheveled from sleep and rubbing her eyes. And grinning as she read the newspaper item.

"They're calling her a '*shero*' in the headline," she told me as I slumped into a chair. "They call you *a friend*. Bummer."

"I don't really care," I said. "I didn't do anything anyway. What about the scarecrow?"

Mom pushed the paper over and I scanned the story. No mention of the scarecrow. It just said that *Buddy Dalton, a stalwart of the Bridgewood community, was chasing a possible intruder from his property at the time of his collapse. Monica Buckley and a friend happened upon the scene. Young Monica leapt into action and likely saved Buddy's life with her composure and quick thinking as she performed* CPR *on him.*

"Wow. Now I *really* feel like crap," I told them.

Mom patted my hand. I hated it when she got all sympathetic like that.

"Maybe you should take a first-aid course, Dylan. They offer them at the rec center."

"Yeah, maybe," I said. "I'm not hungry. I think I'll just grab a granola bar and ride my bike to school today."

"Ride?" Mom said. "But it's raining out."

"Don't worry, okay? I'm meeting up with Cory. It's just a couple of miles. I'll be fine."

I grabbed the granola bar, my windbreaker and my backpack and left without another word. And felt their eyes boring into the back of my head as I shut the door.

Monica avoided me again all day Wednesday. It was messing me up inside, and I couldn't quite figure out why she was so mad. Because I couldn't help out when Buddy Dalton collapsed? Or because I didn't call 9-1-1 fast enough? Or because I didn't tell the truth about what happened or about the movie we were making? I figured it was most likely all of the above.

At least people turned out in droves for the casting call after school. All except for Monica. Cory and I had set up a table on the auditorium floor, and we each had a notebook. All the kids gathered around in the seats, yapping nonstop about how awesome this was going to be. I sure hoped they were right.

First we took down everyone's names. Then I explained the scarecrow part, which everyone thought was totally cool. Some of the kids even gave zombie moans of approval. I told them not to worry about their scarecrow stuffing. Cory and I would be ready with bags of straw to stuff into their shirts at the staging place in the park on Saturday. Cory had gotten hold of a pile of straw from his uncle's farm.

Some of the kids had dressed the part, in tattered clothes and lots of gore. They wanted to be zombies, and Cory and I had no problem with that. They didn't even have to audition. But everyone else did, and we handed them each a sample of the script so they could practice before we called them to the stage. Then we auditioned them in groups of four. We had everyone read some lines from the script and then zombie-walk across the stage. That way we could figure out who would be best to play the roles of the humans and who would make the best zombie scarecrows.

HUMAN ONE

I got a feeling this is gonna be a really long night.

ZOMBIES

(walking and slathering)

Ahhhrrrgh. Ahhhrrrgh.

HUMAN TWO

(panicking)

We need to figure out a way to stop them. Or else we're totally doomed!

ZOMBIES

(same as above)

HUMAN ONE
Okay, chill out for a second.
I think I got a plan.

ZOMBIES
(same as above)

HUMAN TWO
(still panicking)
Well, I sure hope it's a freakin'
good one, dude!

Yep, pretty simple. I didn't mention that I still hadn't worked out the finer details of the plan, or the ending. But everyone who tried out was totally into it. Henry and Helena showed up. So did Charlie the jerk, and they all brought friends. Garrett was there, too, with a few guys from his football team. But it didn't matter now because Monica wasn't there to scowl, though I wished she was. Even Tim Dalton showed up, which was weird since his granddad had had a heart attack on Monday.

"Hey," I said as he and his friend Rick Smith came up to our table. They were a couple of goofy grade-niners who thought they were cool. "Your grandpa doing okay now? Is he still in the hospital?"

"Guess so," he said, and then half scowled. "I think he was getting home today."

Weird.

"So Tim and I just want to be zombie scarecrows," Rick told us. "Do we still need to read lines? 'Cause I seriously suck at reading."

"Okay, cool, if you don't want lines, you can be scarecrows," I said, and they high-fived each other and walked away.

The last one to audition was Garrett.

"This is totally sick, dudes," he said just before his reading. "My friends have always wanted to be in a play but didn't want to learn all those lines. They want to be zombies. But I would *love* to be one of the humans."

"Well, there are only two main humans, and a few sidekick humans with minimal lines," I explained. "So we'll have to see how you do."

"Sweet," he said. I didn't think I'd ever seen him so pumped for anything outside of a football game.

"Okay, so read for us, Garrett," Cory told him.

I was shocked. Garrett did a great job. I figured even Monica would have been impressed. And since she wasn't on board anymore, I got to make the decision.

"Okay, you can be Human One, and your friends are zombie scarecrows," I told him, not even checking with Cory first. He knew exactly why. It was always wise to be on the good side of Garrett.

And Garrett was so thrilled to get the part that he did a fist pump.

While everyone waited, Cory and I put our heads together. Ten minutes later I made the announcement.

"So we've chosen Garrett to be Human One," I told them. He and his buds whooped, but there were a few grumbles from the rest of the kids. "And Helena will be Human Two." I heard her clapping, along with a few other Theater Arts kids.

"Henry will be the main zombie," Cory told them.

"Cool," we heard Henry say. "I was hoping for that."

Then we told them who the rest of the humans and zombies would be. Everyone had a part, and there were more than twenty-five kids there. Which was perfect. Before they left, I gave the four-page script to everyone who had lines.

"There's one more page, but you can't have it until Saturday, when we meet in the park at five," I told them. "'Cause that would be a spoiler." *Yeah, right. Spoiler*.

Everyone was good with that. They all looked at their scripts, nodding and laughing and yacking about how epic this would be.

I was sure glad they bought my spoiler story, because it was a great way to stall for time until I figured out the perfect ending.

We got the main characters onstage after that and did a quick read through, and walked them through their parts a few times. Since the drama kids were practically pros, they nearly had their lines learned before we even finished. Except for Charlie. He didn't have any lines because I made that jerk a zombie scarecrow.

Before we all went our separate ways, we set up a text-messaging system to make sure everyone turned up on time Saturday. Pretty much everyone went home happy around five o'clock, including Cory.

But not including miserable me.

Chapter Four

At least the rain had stopped and Cory and I didn't have to bike home in it. Just as we were crossing town, Nicole pulled up in her cruiser. She was *always* at work! Her huge police dog, Prince, was panting over her shoulder in the backseat.

"Hey, guys," she said. "Everything okay?"

"Not answering that question without my lawyer present," I told her, and she smirked.

She motioned me over to the car, and I leaned in from my bike seat and let Prince lick my hand. She let me get away with it, so I figured she needed something from me.

"It happened again on Buddy Dalton's street last night," she told me, watching Cory over my shoulder. "This time *two* jerks pitched a pumpkin through the door when the people answered."

"But why did they even *answer*? It's okay. I told Cory. He won't blab anything."

Nicole rolled her eyes. "Of course you did. And who knows why they answered. Folks are way too trusting in Bridgewood. Almost never lock their doors. Have you heard anything around school? Any rumors? Anything at all?"

"So now I'm a stool pigeon instead of a suspect?" I said. Cory started laughing.

Nicole smirked again. "Whatever works," she said. "So?"

"Nope. Nothing. Oh, wait. Mr. Dalton's grandson Tim showed up to audition for our movie this afternoon. That seemed weird."

"Dylan, you're not supposed to be making that…" she began, and I held up one hand.

"Relax. I took what you told me seriously, you know. Everything will be fine."

"Hope so," she said with narrowed eyes. "Yeah, Timmy Dalton. Funny kid. No love lost between him and his grandpa, from what I've heard. I think Buddy's closer to his step-grandson than he is to his flesh-and-blood one. Poor fellow's lost *two* wives to cancer already."

"Wow, that sucks," I said.

"Keep your feelers up, okay, guys?" Nicole said, then drove off.

"You kind of lied to her again," Cory said.

"That wasn't *technically* a lie," I told him. "And everything *will* be fine. Especially after we put my plan into action tonight. See ya at seven."

We high-fived each other and rode off in separate directions.

When I got to the apartment, feeling starved for the first time in almost two days, Gran *wasn't* there waiting for me. Neither was my supper. And I had to leave again in an hour.

For a second I was really scared. Because Gran was almost always on the sofa knitting and watching TV, or cooking something awesome, or talking on the phone. I hunted all over the apartment, which took one minute. I was half afraid

I'd find her passed out, like what had happened to Buddy Dalton. And I wouldn't know how to save her. Maybe that first-aid course wasn't such a bad idea.

I was about to call Mom at Rocky's Roadhouse when I heard the key rattle in the lock. And there was Gran, a big smile on her face. And a freshly roasted chicken from the supermarket.

"Awesome! I'm ravenous," I said, taking the bag from her. "How come you didn't cook the chicken yourself, anyway?"

The aroma was killing me. I could have eaten it all. There was a baguette and a bag of premade salad too. Which was strange. Gran hated wasting money on prepared stuff like this.

"Funny you should ask," she said as she hung up her coat. "I spent the afternoon with Buddy. He got home from the hospital today. I baked cookies and took them over after lunch."

"And you're just getting back *now*?" I said as I ripped into the chicken.

Gran gave me the sideways look. "Save some for me," she said. "Oh, I'm finished knitting Monica's socks. You can tell her that. The next pair is for Buddy."

Instead of answering, I chomped into a chicken leg. And wondered what the heck was going on with my grandmother. Because I'd never seen a smile so wide on her face. *Ever.*

I did *not* want to think about who Monica had been sitting with at lunchtime in the cafeteria again that day. Or how close together they'd been sitting, all by themselves. Or how close their faces had been. Or how much I'd wanted to punch Charlie Wells when he'd come to the audition that afternoon. So making up an excuse to leave the house around seven that evening was a good distraction.

"I'm just going over to Cory's for a while, Gran," I called as I headed for the door.

"You're hardly ever home these days, Dylan," she said over her shoulder. "And I never know what you're up to anymore either. Be careful, okay? I can never seem to stop worrying."

"Promise, Gran," I said. These days she hardly ever let me leave without taking a potshot.

As I biked over to Cory's in the dusky light, my tires splashed through puddles that I didn't try to avoid. The neighborhood looked even creepier on a cool, misty evening like this, with all those soaking-wet scarecrows posed on the porches and lawns. It was the perfect backdrop for my awesome plan to bring down the troublemaker. I had a hunch that the pumpkin vandal, or possibly even vandals, planned on striking each night before Halloween. And that he, or they, had targeted Buddy Dalton's street, for some reason. Now that he was home from the hospital, they might even hit up his house again. Which is why I had a scarecrow costume, black Halloween makeup from the dollar store and a camera stashed in my backpack, and why Cory had the same things in his.

He was waiting for me at the park, in the shadows of the concession kiosk that was boarded up for the off-season.

"You got everything?" I asked as I rode my bike over to him. "Did you hide those folding camp chairs in the right place?"

"Yep, on the way here. Behind those bushes on Beechwood Lane," he said. "Good thing it's foggy and almost dark—*nobody* saw me. I grabbed a pair of my dad's old trackpants and a hoodie. And one of his fishing hats. Our video camera too. How 'bout you?"

He started hauling the clothes out of his backpack and pulling them on over his own.

"Yeah, that was a challenge," I told him. Then I opened my backpack and held up the stuff I'd found in a zippered bag at the back of the hall closet.

"Seriously," he said and started laughing. "How *old* is that crap anyway?"

"I have no clue," I said, pulling on a tattered wool trench coat and some sort of a Sherlock Holmes hat. "I think they used to belong to my grandpa, and he died a few years ago. So give me a break, okay?"

"You smell like mothballs," he said as we both spread black makeup on our faces.

"Like I care. Okay, we gotta book it now. We don't want to miss 'em."

"But what if Officer Vance is staking them out too?" Cory asked as we ran through the shadows toward Beechwood Lane.

"We've got to take that chance," I said. "Try to beat these suckers at their own game so they get caught. And then maybe Nicole won't freak out when we make our zombie movie on Halloween night. Anyway, I'm sure she won't park there. Might be cruising the 'hood though."

Sure enough, just as we reached Buddy Dalton's street, we spotted head-lights moving toward us, extremely slowly. I yanked Cory behind some bushes before the car could get too close. And yep, it was Nicole in her cruiser.

"Whew, close one. We should be good for a bit now. Let's go!" I said.

In the next few minutes we set up the chairs in front of bushes on the lawns of two properties across from Buddy Dalton's place, out of view of the homeowners. It was perfect. The closest streetlight was a few houses down, and there was enough of an orange glow that we'd be able to get good footage from our stakeout chairs.

"Okay," I told Cory. "Just sit there like one of those stuffed scarecrows, and don't move. As soon as you see *anything*, start shooting. Trust me, they'll be too busy to notice when we hold up our cameras. And keep your hat down low."

Cory nodded and sank into his chair, and I ran over to settle into mine. Then I sat shivering in the October chill, hoping this plan would work out. Fifteen minutes later, Nicole did another drive-by. I sucked in my breath when I saw her car. But she cruised right on past without even noticing us. Her head was turned toward Buddy's house when she went by, as though she was checking up on him. His porch light was on, but the house was dark.

As soon as she rounded the corner and was out of sight, I saw two figures sneak along the street. They must have been waiting for the right moment, like we were. Well, the first thing I saw was the glowing jack-o'-lantern that looked as if it were floating in the dark. Which totally spooked me. That was when I turned my camera on and started shooting.

The scarecrows kept to the shadows. Just like the one I'd seen the other night, they wore wide straw hats and baggy old scarecrow clothes. The taller one was carrying the pumpkin. I zoomed in as they approached. They were five houses away from us. Four houses. Three houses. My heart was in my throat, and the camera was shaking in my hand. They were only two houses away.

And then the front door of the house beside Buddy's burst open. A man came flying out.

"I'll get you, you sick little brats," he yelled and started chasing them.

The tall masked scarecrow pitched his pumpkin at the guy, and then they both started running. Really fast. I followed them with my camera. I got it all, every single bit, in that orange streetlight glow. And then the best thing happened. The short scarecrow's straw hat flew off as they were zooming past me. And I got a head shot and gasped.

The idiot wasn't even wearing a mask. It was Buddy's grandson, Tim Dalton!

Chapter Five

I kept on shooting until they were out of sight. I kept recording as the furious neighbor shook his fist at the empty street where the scarecrows had been. Then he picked up Tim's straw hat and, cursing, went back into his house. And I sat there breathing hard for a few minutes, until I figured it was safe to move.

"Cory," I called in a loud whisper. "Can you even *believe* this? Did you get it all?"

"Yep," he called back. "Timmy freaking Dalton!"

"Let's get out of here fast and check out our footage at your place," I said.

We stashed the chairs in the bushes, then hoofed it along Beechwood Lane toward the park to pick up our bikes and backpacks. But we stopped dead at the park entrance.

"Oh *crap*," I said.

"*Double* crap," Cory said.

Nicole's cruiser was parked in front of the kiosk. In the dim park light, we could see her leaning against her cruiser door. Staring right at us. She had Prince on a leash.

"We're toast," I said.

"Should we just try and make a run for it?" Cory said.

"Yeah, that'll work," I told him. "Give your head a shake."

"Hi, boys," she called. "Are you having fun tonight? I think you dropped your pumpkin back there." She held up a hunk of pumpkin flesh. God, she was good at her job.

"It wasn't us, Nicole," I said, starting toward her and hoping Cory would follow. He did, but not as fast.

She was shaking her head when we reached her.

"Lock up your bikes, grab your backpacks, and climb in the backseat, guys," she said. "I hope your parents won't ground you for life." Long scary pause. "I sure hope you don't get charged with attempted murder either."

And that was about when Cory started crying.

If it hadn't been for our cameras and Buddy's neighbor's misplaced glasses, we would have been doomed. But with his vision blurred, Mr. Loughlin really couldn't see what the scarecrow vandals had been wearing as he chased them. He couldn't distinguish between them and us when he tried to describe them to Nicole. Plus we both still had our hats. And neither of them was straw. At the cop shop we handed our cameras over to Nicole. She got to see the footage of Tim and his friend—who was smart enough to wear a mask—at the very moment they were doing their dirty work. We were totally off the hook. And almost sort-of heroes.

Of course, Tim ratted out the other scarecrow, Rick Smith. Tim also told Nicole that he couldn't find a mask at home and had pulled his straw hat down low to hide his face. Guess he didn't figure on having to run so fast that the hat would blow off. Real good plan, Timmy.

But why? *Why* would they do it? Especially to Tim's own grandfather!

Rick denied the whole thing, we found out from Nicole on Thursday, my mom's day off. She was visiting Mom when Cory and I got home from school.

"You have no idea how lucky you and Cory were," Nicole told us over mugs of tea.

Cory just sat there wide-eyed, holding his mug and nodding.

"You were pretty lucky yourself," I reminded her. "That the two of us were there with our cameras. Right, Cory?"

Cory stopped nodding and stared at Nicole like he was afraid to hear her answer.

"Huh, that's debatable," Nicole said, shaking her head and trying not to grin.

"Bold thing," Gran said, poking me with a skinny knitting needle.

"Ouch! Watch where you're sticking that, Gran!"

"Jeez, Dylan," Mom said. "Are you *kidding* me? You think *you two* solved this thing?"

"It's true," I told them. "You'd still be looking for them if it wasn't for us, right, Nicole? So it's okay to do our movie now. Right?"

She nodded and sighed and grinned some more. "But don't breathe a word about Tim," she warned. "The family doesn't want Buddy to know it was him. It would break his heart."

"No doubt," I said. I wondered again why anyone would do something so dumb.

"Little jerk," Gran grumbled. "I'd like to get my hands on that kid."

By the look of fury on her face, I figured Timmy Dalton should be watching his back.

And better yet, the photographer from the local paper came by to take a picture of Cory and me later on Thursday evening.

"You again, huh," he said. "Why am I not surprised? Where's your girlfriend, Monica Buckley? I hear you were with her the other night when she did CPR on Buddy Dalton."

Heat prickled the back of my neck, and I felt myself flushing. My clearly *ex*-girlfriend had totally avoided me at school again that day. And had sat with Charlie again too. I tried to cover up. "So why didn't you print my name?" I said. "Why was I just *a friend*?"

"Hey, give someone else a turn to be hero for a change," he said, grinning as he clicked his camera a few times. "At least Cory got in on it this time. Photo will be in the paper tomorrow. Couple of heroes, huh? You'll have to share some hero space with Mr. Loughlin."

After that, we ordered a deluxe pizza to celebrate the coolness of not being in trouble. And doing something useful to help out Nicole. I should have felt really good for the rest of that evening. Mom, Nicole, Cory and I watched one of Mom's fave campy flicks, *Army of Darkness*, on DVD. (Gran took a pass when she heard the title.) And we chowed down on a huge pile of caramel corn. But I couldn't enjoy any of it.

Because down deep, I couldn't stop thinking about…yep, Monica Buckley.

And sure enough, on Friday morning there we were on the front page. Holding our cameras and grinning like a couple of idiots. The headline read *Local boys with cameras help bust pumpkin vandals*.

Mom was smiling over her coffee. Gran was smiling too. Wider than usual.

"I'm going over to see Buddy at lunch-time today," she said. "I made him some nice thick tuna sandwiches on crusty bread. Can't wait to hear his take on this thing."

It was a good bet he was getting lots of mayo and chopped-up apples in *his* sandwich.

"What's up with that, Mom?" my mom asked Gran. "You got a thing for Buddy Dalton now, or what?"

I'm pretty sure Gran started blushing. And she was speechless for the first time *ever*.

Cory and I rode our bikes to school to avoid the attention on the bus. I was proud of what we'd done. But kids had started to call me Sherlock Holmes even before this latest incident. I was already sick of hearing it. As soon as we rode up to the school, though, someone yelled out a window, "Nice work crackin' the case, Sherlock."

And during the announcements, the principal announced that, yes, we had a couple more heroes at the school this morning. But he didn't go into detail like he had with Monica on Tuesday. The *Bridgewood Weekly* couldn't print the vandals' names since they were juveniles.

I wondered if Tim Dalton and Rick Smith would show up at school that day. How could they face anyone after what they'd done? But if nobody knew who the pumpkin vandals actually were, their *not* showing up would make it obvious.

I'd mentioned all of this to Cory on the bike ride to school. We'd decided to keep our feelers out throughout the morning. We'd find out what everyone else knew, then compare notes in the cafeteria at lunchtime.

Lots of kids came up to me in class and in the hallways and asked the burning question. *So who was it, Dylan*, I heard over and over again. And all I did was shrug.

Tim Dalton *did* come to school. He treated me like I was invisible, which didn't matter because that was how I always treated him. He'd been a whiner in middle school, from what I remembered. He had an overprotective mom who dropped him off at school every day instead of making him take the bus with the rest of us. And back then, he'd picked his nose in public. And *ate* it! He'd never had many friends, for obvious reasons.

Only one person said something *interesting* to me that morning. That was Rick Smith.

"Wasn't me, Dillweed," he murmured as he passed me in the hall. That was Garrett's favorite name for me, which Rick had probably overheard at middle school. How totally lame.

"Whatever," I muttered back. "Tell it to the judge."

He turned so red I thought his head would explode as he stalked off.

"Nothing, zippo, nada," I told Cory when I plopped down at the table in the cafeteria.

"Me either," Cory said. "Nobody knows who it was. Everybody wants to though."

I unwrapped my sandwich. It was a big thick tuna salad on crusty bread with lots of mayo and chopped-up apple. And there were four gingersnaps. And a couple of Clementine oranges, and a ziplock bag of jujubes, Gran's favorite candy. It seemed I was in her good books again.

But nothing really mattered that day. Because Monica didn't even show up in the cafeteria at lunch. And neither did Charlie Wells. I was antsy the entire time, and Cory could tell. He kept watching me and shaking his head.

"Okay, so I know I have the hots for Ivy Adams. And I know I check her out whenever I get the chance. There's at least a little payoff. Yesterday in the hallway she actually *smiled* at me, so I'm hoping for *that* today too. But dude! You look like a sad puppy. Monica is *so* done with you. Get *over* it."

"Shut up, Cory," I said. "I'll catch you later, okay? And let you know when I come up with a cool ending for our movie." Then I did a glum zombie walk right out of the cafeteria. I shuffled along the hallway and through the double doors into blinding October sunshine.

Chapter Six

And that was when I caught Charlie and Monica in the middle of a kiss.

They were under the big maple tree on the front lawn of the school. Right in front of everybody. Including me. So I turned around and ran straight back into the school.

For the rest of that afternoon I felt sick. I rode my bike home before last period so I wouldn't have to face anyone in the halls. I didn't care if the attendance office called to report me. It couldn't make me feel any worse than I already did. Nothing could. No matter how mad at me Mom and Gran got, no matter how hard I got lectured or how long I got grounded. Nothing would hurt me as much as seeing Monica Buckley getting kissed by that stupid Charlie Wells. Maybe Cory was right. Maybe it was time for me to forget about Monica. I needed to get over her, since she was clearly done with me.

I was feeling bruised from the inside out when I walked through the apartment door. And Gran wasn't home. I guessed she was still hanging out with Buddy. Even my grandmother had a boyfriend now. I had nobody, and I didn't want anyone but Monica. I dropped my backpack at the door, went straight to my room, flopped on my bed and instantly conked out.

Until someone started shaking my shoulder.

"Why are my father's coat and hat lying on the closet floor?" Gran said in my ear.

"What?" I sat up, rubbing my eyes. "Those are *your* father's things? No wonder they stink like mothballs!"

"*Yes*. And that's all I have left of him. They're *your* legacy too. Was that your scarecrow costume the other night? Honestly, Dylan. Do you have straw for brains, or what?"

Hmm. Sometimes I wondered that myself.

"By the way. You took the wrong lunch bag this morning. That sandwich was meant for Edward." She was still looming over me and glaring.

"Who the heck is Edward?" I asked. "*Another* one of your boyfriends?"

"Dylan!" She was half smiling. "That's Buddy's real name. I call him

78

that sometimes. You were *supposed* to take the leftover chicken and bread for lunch."

"Wow, sorry about that. Day-old chicken on stale bread wasn't good enough for *Edward*, I guess. I'm sure your *boyfriend* has food at home though."

"Look, I told Chuck Wells that I'd bring Edward his lunch today. So I had to stop at Rocky's Roadhouse for some Reuben sandwiches." She rolled her eyes and tsk-tsked.

"And *who* is Chuck Wells? You're confusing sometimes, Gran." I sighed loudly.

"It's Ed—Buddy's stepson. Buddy married Chuck's mother after his first wife died. Chuck still looks out for Buddy, even though his mom passed away a few years back. He's a *very* nice man."

Suddenly I was wide awake.

"Is that Charlie Wells's *dad*? So you mean Buddy Dalton is Charlie's *step-granddad*?"

"Correct," Gran said. "And maybe you should make your own lunches now. I'll start your supper. Not that you deserve it." When she winked, I knew she was joking, sort of.

Gran left my room. And I sat there on the edge of my bed, thinking about how much I loathed Charlie Wells, until our supper was ready. It was wieners and canned beans. Talk about slacking off in the kitchen, all because of her new boyfriend! I didn't dare say that out loud.

Later that evening Cory called to find out if I was still mad. And to see if I'd figured anything out for our movie on Saturday. Guys don't stay mad at each other for long though. So my answer was no and no again.

"You mean you haven't come up with anything?" he yelped into my ear.

"We shoot *tomorrow*! All those kids will show up in their costumes, and we won't..."

"Then *you* think of something," I told him. "I've got too much other junk on my mind."

"Sorry, I got nothing," he said. "Not as creative as you are. Don't read so much either."

"What*ever*," I said. "Maybe we'll just wing it."

"We can't have random zombie scarecrows wandering through town. The humans have to figure out how to stop them. Or it'll suck big-time."

"Okay, so let me think a bit more then," I said and hung up on him.

That night I couldn't fall asleep, I guess because of my afternoon zonk-out. So I was lying there trying not to think about Monica and Charlie at the same time I was trying to come up with an ending for our movie. I'd slept for a bit when I heard Mom come in from her shift at Rocky's. And I started thinking some more.

Straw for brains. That's what Gran had said to me. I knew what she really meant. I thought of the scarecrow in *The Wizard of Oz*, the character that turned out to be the smartest. He had straw for brains but was terrified of a lit match. And flames freaked him out.

Flames. Of course. "That's *it*," I said out loud.

I was so pumped I dialed Cory's cell-phone number right away.

"Dylan? I was asleep, you *jerk*," he mumbled when he answered.

"I've *got* it," I told him. "Meet me at the dollar store at ten."

"Thanks for waking me up, dude," Cory said when we met at Dollarama on Saturday morning.

It had dawned a perfect fall day, cool and bright and not a chance of rain. *Dawn of the Dead*, I couldn't help but think on my way to meet Cory. One of Mom's other favorite undead flicks. *The George A. Romero version from 1978, of course*, she always said. Not *the remake*.

"Hey, you're the one who kept bugging me to think of something. Guess I work better under pressure. Great ending though, isn't it?"

As we parked our bikes, Cory grinned at me. "Not sure. You haven't told me yet."

"You mean I didn't blab it last night? I guess I was half-asleep. It's epic!"

I told him while we shopped for the rest of our props. And he liked it too.

After we'd paid, we rode our bikes back to Cory's house to print the rest of the script. We didn't have a printer at the apartment. An unnecessary frill,

Mom said. I could print at the school library, she said.

As we wheeled along the busy main street, two bikes approached from the opposite direction. When we were close enough, I realized it was Charlie and Tim.

"Great," I said. "My two favorite people. Let's turn before we meet up with them, okay?"

But it was too late. They'd already seen us.

"Hey, Dillweed," Tim yelled. "How's it goin'?" What a *dork*.

"Bite me, dork," I told him as they rode past us.

"Don't you mean *Sherlock*, Tim?" Charlie called over his shoulder, then laughed at his dumb joke. "Your ex-girlfriend's an awesome kisser, by the way." And they were gone.

I swear I instantly started to boil inside my skin.

"Couple of weenies," Cory said when he saw my face. "Forget about 'em, Dylan."

But I'd already turned my bike around to follow them.

"Seriously, dude," Cory said, following me. "It's so not worth it."

"You don't know how much I hate that he was kissing her," I growled as I started pedaling harder. "I'd love to punch his lights out."

"But he's way bigger than you," Cory said, trying to catch up. "*And* me!"

"But there're two of us," I told him.

"And two of them," Cory reminded me. "It won't end well."

"Tim doesn't count. He's puny. He'll be too busy picking his nose."

"Yep, that's true," Cory agreed.

We let them get just far enough ahead that they wouldn't notice us following them. I was feeling breathless, my heart pounding hard, an unfamiliar fury surging from somewhere inside me. Somewhere I'd thought was mostly dead. It felt pretty alive right now though.

And then they turned onto Beechwood Lane. Buddy Dalton's street.

"Crap. They're going to visit their grandfather, I bet," I said.

"What?" Cory said. "Am I missing something?"

"You sure are," I said, then told him what Gran had told me the day before.

"Nice grandsons," Cory said with a scowl. "What a couple of dweebs. I wonder if he even likes them. Guess you have to like your own flesh and blood though, huh?"

"Not necessarily. And anyway, Charlie isn't blood. But he *is* a total jerk."

We rode past Buddy's house. Their bikes were dumped on his front lawn. And they were about to go inside when Charlie spotted us.

"Hey, Sherlock! You followed us here? Are ya jealous of Mon and me? Or crushing on me like all the other girls?" He gave a loud laugh, sort of like a donkey. Or more like a jackass.

"Yeah, the Dillweed probably is," goofball Timmy piped up.

Mon? Nobody called her Mon. She hated that nickname. I stopped my bike in the middle of the road and put both feet on the ground. My hands turned into fists.

"Cool it," Cory warned me. "Their grandfather just had a heart attack, remember."

"Duh! I know," I growled. "But I can't do *nothing*." Then I knew exactly what to do.

"Okay, you know what, you jerks?" I said. "Don't bother showing up in the park today. You're out of the movie."

"No kidding, dork," Tim said. "You really think I was still coming?"

Charlie's face went hard.

"Well, I'm still showing up," he told us. "I need this for my volunteer community service."

"Seriously?" Cory laughed. "This doesn't count for community service, you idiot."

"Nice try, loser," I said. Then we got back on our bikes and rode away.

When I took a chance and looked back, Charlie was standing in the middle of the road, giving me the finger. With both hands.

Chapter Seven

I had no regrets for cutting Charlie from the movie. In fact, I felt amazing for a change, especially after that little adrenaline rush in front of Buddy's place.

That afternoon Cory messaged the main cast on his cell phone. He reminded them to text everyone else to show up on time and in costume. They'd blend well with all the other Halloween madness happening in town that day. I thought it would be a challenge to get Gran to let me wear my great-grandpa's clothes again. But she didn't put up a fight.

"Take good care of them," she said as I headed out to meet Cory in the park at four thirty. "If you get *anything* on that coat, you'll have to pay for the cleaning bill yourself."

"I will guard this stinky old coat with my life, Gran."

"Don't get smart. Maybe I'll see you out there on the streets. I'm going over to Edward's to help him hand out candy. We're even carving his pumpkin first. And look." She held up a pair of gray, navy and maroon-striped socks. "He's getting them today. That reminds me. When's Monica coming over to pick up her pair?"

Sucker punch to the gut. "Not sure, Gran," I told her, and looked the other way. But not before I saw the look on her face that said *It's over, isn't it? Poor you.*

Gran was smiling as I said goodbye. It was cool to see her getting out of the house and being so happy these days. Mom and Brent had already headed for Rocky's Roadhouse, where they were helping set up for a Halloween shindig that evening. They went as an undead bride and groom. Brent had brought the costumes and professional makeup from a rental place in the city. They looked amazing when they left the apartment, holding hands. Like that crazy scene from *Beetlejuice*.

I headed for the park on my bike, backpack over my shoulders and the camera, script and props stashed inside. It was almost time for the Big Reveal. Everyone seemed to be outside, raking leaves, riding bikes, playing with their kids. And perfecting their scarecrow displays for the judging tour the next day.

It sounded like one huge shriek coming from all the excited kids running around in costumes, having sword fights, parading glittery dresses or unleashing inner monsters. All hyped for Halloween. It kind of made me miss those days. I used to love running in big rubber boots as a cape flapped behind me, being my favorite superhero of the week.

Cory was waiting for me, sitting on a picnic table and grinning as I rode up.

"I am so pumped for this," he said.

"You got your camera, right?"

"Well *duh*," he said. "I hope you're good at cutting this flick. If I try and edit, I'm sure I'll mess it up big-time."

"No worries," I said. "I love editing. It's almost better than shooting, I think. I picked a great soundtrack called *Danse Macabre*, by some dead composer. You should check it out."

"God, you're such a freakin' geek," he said, then rolled his eyes and snorted.

Before five, the cast started turning up. And their zombie makeup was so perfect, it was hard to tell who anyone was. That is, until Human One came up and punched me on the arm.

"Hey, Dillweed! Thanks for letting me be a main human, man. Hah! Hu*man* man," Garrett said. "I know my lines and I will totally rock this role. Rock 'n' roll! Hah! Get it?"

There was no way I was going to try and explain the different spellings.

By five o'clock, most of the kids were sprawled on park benches and picnic tables and going over their lines. Cory dumped out the bags of straw, and the zombie scarecrows stuffed their necks and tattered sleeves. They were excited like crazy and already in character. They stumbled around, moaning and slathering and crashing into each other. They dripped gore as they chased down the human characters, jerking in that strange spastic way that's so creepy in all the movies. Some were even chewing on bloody severed arms and legs. It was spectacular.

But I started to get nervous when a couple of little kids screamed and ran away. And when a couple of others burst into tears as their parents ushered them from the play structure, shaking their heads and frowning at us. Then I saw Nicole coming in her street clothes. Well, more like cowboy clothes. She was holding hands with her new "cowboy" boyfriend, Greg.

"I think you might be freaking out the town," she said, looking at all the zombies. She was smiling, though, which was a good sign. "Everything's cool here, right, guys?"

"You bet it is, Sheriff," I told her. "Where'd you two leave your horses tied up anyway?"

Greg smirked. "Funny guy. Just like you said, Nic."

"He's my godson," she told Greg. "It's my job to keep him out of trouble. It's not working very well. It's my night off, Dylan. I'd like to keep it that way, okay?"

"No problem," I said as they walked off. Cory didn't say a word the whole time. He just watched wide-eyed, like he was afraid of her. It was too funny.

"Okay, let's do this!" I clapped my hands to get everybody's attention. And wow, they all stopped and walked right over. I spotted another zombie scarecrow hurrying across the park. "Hold it—one more person." Then I realized who it was.

Monica? My throat kind of closed on me. She didn't come over. She sat at a distance on a park bench and watched us and gave me a little finger flutter when I stared.

"Dylan. Let's go!" Cory nudged me hard in the ribs.

"Right. Is everyone ready to hear the ending? Because it is *extremely* cool!"

When I explained the last scene, they all clapped and cheered like crazy. Then Cory handed out the plastic lighters we'd bought at the dollar store. And I handed out the brilliant last page of the script to everybody.

"Got one for me?" Monica said when I passed her bench. "I totally love your ending, by the way." There was a gory, gaping hole in her cheek—most excellent makeup job.

"Last I heard, you weren't coming to this thing," I said and kept on walking. Then felt her arm on my shoulder.

"I changed my mind. Is that all right?"

Her soft, sweet voice made something like a balloon start expanding in my chest. "So how come?" I said.

"I'll explain later," she told me. "Um…I can help you edit. If you still want me to. I'm good with sound."

"Hmm. Maybe I'll think about it," I said and handed her the last page.

I knew I wouldn't have to think about it very long. I just needed to know why. I stared at the assembled cast, and then I cleared my voice.

"Okay, so picture the very last scene. Before we zoom in on the jack-o'-lantern in the window. All the humans chase the zombie scarecrows out of town. With *these* lighters."

I lit mine and held it up in the air. The cast raised theirs, cheered and whistled.

"So what's that supposed to do again?" a zombie scarecrow asked in a slow voice.

I sighed. "Haven't you seen *The Wizard of Oz*? Scarecrows are afraid of fire. So zombie scarecrows would be too. Like I already explained."

"But they're already *dead*. So why would they be afraid of a lighter?" the same kid said.

"They're zombie/scarecrow hybrids though," Cory reminded him. "They'd still be scared of fire."

I could see Monica laughing on the bench, and I grinned.

"It's called *suspension of disbelief*," I told the guy. "So don't worry about it. I wonder if George Romero had to go through this when he shot the *Evil Dead* series."

We started with the opening scenes, when the scarecrows in the park start morphing into zombies as darkness sets in on Halloween. This all happens because of a strange porcine virus they picked up from moldy straw. Pigs and humans are closely related, after all. So it wasn't *that* much of a stretch.

Garrett hadn't been kidding. He knew his lines perfectly. Some of the other kids, not so much. But every time somebody blew a line, Garrett knew it and prompted them. I couldn't believe it, and I actually high-fived him at one point. Even Monica looked impressed. In fact, we wouldn't have gotten through those opening shots so fast if it wasn't for my nemesis Garrett.

While Cory and I were shooting, that curtain of darkness started to fall. Parents and older kids in costume crossed the park. Most of them stopped to watch. I could tell they were mesmerized. Even Monica was into it. She was stumbling around with the other zombie scarecrows. Actually playing a part in our movie.

I could not believe how well this whole thing was going. I felt as happy as a little kid on Halloween, for the first time in ages.

"We are killing this," I said to Cory, who was filming with his camera too. "We rock!"

It was almost dark. And almost time to move the cast to the main street for the epic zombie scarecrow march out of town. Awesome.

Chapter Eight

Before that, though, we had to shoot the final lines of *Rise of the Zombie Scarecrows*. And even though I'd handed out the last page only an hour ago, it took only three takes.

MAIN ZOMBIE (Henry)
(jerking, hiding eyes and groaning)
NOOOOOOOOOO!

The other zombies MOAN and GROAN as they all turn away from the flames.

HUMAN TWO (Helena)
My god! You were right! It's actually freakin' working!

HUMAN ONE (Garrett)
I told you there's always a good reason to carry a lighter.

HUMAN TWO
Yeah, right. Last time you said that, you started a grass fire.

HUMAN ONE
Hey, don't judge me. I'm only human, you know.

Humans One and Two high-five as other humans all laugh. Zombie scarecrows MOAN and GROAN with fear and act confused.

HUMANS ONE and TWO
(holding lighters up)
Okay, let's finish this thing!

All humans start YELLING and shaking their hockey sticks and baseball bats. Then, with lighters held high, they chase zombie scarecrows out of town along Main Street.

"Cut!" I yelled. "Excellent! That's a wrap!"

Technically, there was one more scene to shoot, but I'd always wanted to say that. Everybody clapped and whooped. Beside me, Cory sighed. I was about to start herding everyone in the right direction when I had a brainstorm to switch the route of the zombie march.

"Okay, you guys," I shouted. "It's time to move on to 'Main Street' now."

They actually broke character and listened to me. Even Monica, who was chilling with some of her fellow-zombie girlfriends. It felt cool. Usually I was the *last* person anyone ever listened to. Cory stood there with his camera, waiting for instructions.

"Exit stage left?" he said, grinning.

"Nope, we're going the other way. I want to make a detour along Beechwood Lane. And surprise my gran. She's over at Buddy Dalton's place handing out candy tonight."

Yep, Gran's ongoing guilt trip had ground me down. I figured it was time to let her see what I was up to.

Cory grinned wider. "You're totally spying on her, aren't you?"

"I can't even believe you said that." I shook my head. "Okay, everyone, we're going that way." I pointed to the other end of the park. "We're making this a longer zombie march. Humans, raise your weapons and lighters in the air. Zombie scarecrows, let's see major fear of those flames for the grand finale."

"So where do you want me, Mr. Spielberg?" Cory said.

I laughed. "Walking with the zombies as you shoot," I told him. "I'll walk backward, right in front of Henry. And pan around at all the awesome scarecrow scenes on the front lawns too. Stay under the streetlights so we get everything."

It was as if the streets had been designed for our movie. There were jack-o'-lanterns on almost every windowsill and porch. Stuffed scarecrows sprawled everywhere. Not all scarecrows were infected because the porcine virus only reanimated the scarecrows stuffed with pig-tainted straw, of course. As we turned onto Beechwood Lane, I hoped Gran would be out on the porch with Buddy Dalton to witness the spectacle of our zombie parade. I also hoped she wouldn't be scared and think we were a gang of vandals.

It wasn't so easy walking backward with the camera in my hand. Now and then I looked over my shoulder so I wouldn't wipe out on a curb or crash into someone. Most of the little kids were done trick-or-treating by then. And the older ones with stuffed loot bags stopped to watch. Some even joined the gang of humans chasing the zombie scarecrows out of town.

We were five houses away from Buddy's. Four houses. *Please be out there, Gran.* Three houses. Two houses.

"What the heck?" I said. Across the road from Buddy's house, one of our camp chairs was set up again. A big scarecrow was slumped in it. With a lit jack-o'-lantern on its lap. "Cool! The neighbors used one of our chairs!" I called to Cory.

I pointed, and Cory started shooting. Then I looked over at Buddy's house and waved. And dropped my hand really fast, then almost dropped my camera. "*Oh, gross!*"

Buddy and Gran were hugging and kissing out on the porch, right under the light! Gran saw me and waved. "Hey there, Dylan. Having fun? Take good care of that coat, okay?"

I was so stunned, all I could do was gape and wave back. Then I realized I was actually shooting Gran and Buddy instead of the zombie scarecrows. I heard a shout from the crowd, followed by more loud shouts. I pointed the camera at the shambling zombie scarecrows again and tried to blot out what I'd just seen on that porch.

"Dylan, turn around! *Look*," Cory said, pointing to something behind me.

I spun around and kept on shooting. And realized that the scarecrow wasn't in the chair anymore. He was in the middle of the road, arm in the air. Then the jack-o'-lantern was flying straight toward Buddy's front porch. I yelped when it hit the porch railing with a huge splat.

Gram shouted something like "Catch that little jerk." Then she practically jumped off the porch, like she was going to chase him down. Buddy grabbed her arm and hung on to her though. The scarecrow was booking it, right down the middle of Beechwood Lane. Cory and I couldn't chase him with cameras in our hands, so it looked like he was getting away. Gran was wrestling Buddy to break loose.

"Calm down, Lori," he told her in a loud voice. "Let the kids take care of it." Wow, sometimes I forgot my grandmother had a real name.

"Crap," I yelled. "Who *was* that?"

"Wow, check it out, Dylan!" Cory said.

And that was when Human One charged, practically plowing down all the zombie scarecrows in his path.

"Cut! Cut! *Cut*!" I started yelling, but Garrett kept running straight past me, like he was on a football field or something.

Then I realized that Garrett was chasing the guy. And Garrett was a quarterback, so he could run *really* fast. Just as the scarecrow vandal was about to turn the corner, Garrett tackled him and took him down right on somebody's front lawn.

It was totally awesome.

"I got it all, dude," Cory yelled as he ran up to me with his camera.

"Me too," I said. "Best. Halloween. *Ever*."

Then Garrett whipped off the scarecrow vandal's hat and mask. And it was Charlie Wells underneath. His face was all scrunched up like he wanted to cry. I could *not* believe it.

About six kids called 9-1-1 from their cell phones at the same time. Garret sat on the scarecrow until the cruiser zoomed up. Officer Donahue was on the case tonight. By then the whole film cast, along with random neighbors and trick-or-treaters, had gathered around Garrett and Charlie. Gran and Buddy had wandered over. I was afraid Gran might punch him, she was so furious. Charlie still didn't look very happy, trapped on his belly under Garrett's butt. I'm pretty sure there were tears on his face because he'd been busted. And maybe because Garrett was a heavy guy.

"I think you can get off him now," I said.

Garrett just grinned up at me. "I'm enjoying this too much. But if you say so."

"Well, well. Charlie Wells." The officer stared down at him. Charlie covered his face with his hands and then curled up on his side. "All along it was *you* tossing pumpkins on this street. Guess you'd better come with me now."

When Donahue hauled Charlie to the cruiser, Charlie was *really* crying. I felt like clapping, but I resisted the urge. And I only realized Monica was standing beside me when she laced her fingers through mine and squeezed. I didn't squeeze back.

"I'm sorry I overreacted about everything that happened this week, Dylan," she whispered beside my ear.

"You were mad at me for not telling Nicole the truth on Monday night, weren't you?" I said. "About seeing the scarecrow vandal and about the plans for shooting our movie tonight."

"Yeah, so I didn't want to talk to you, to make my point. Then I sat with Charlie at lunch. I guess I was trying to make you jealous too. Very bad move. I don't *like* him. At *all*!"

"But I saw you kissing him that day. In front of the whole school."

"Yuck. Wasn't *my* idea," she told me. "He cornered me against that tree and practically shoved his tongue down my throat. I kneed him good, you know. You missed that part."

Wow. No wonder I was crazy about Monica Buckley. I kissed her gently, and she kissed me back. When I looked over at Gran, she smiled and gave me the thumbs-up.

Chapter Nine

Right after Officer Donahue got Charlie in the squad car and drove off, we called it a night.

"We have great footage, everyone. You can all go home and finish partying. I'll let you know when there's a screening," I told them.

Everyone clapped, and then the crowd dispersed. Only Monica, Cory and I were left standing there with Buddy Dalton and Gran. I could hardly even look at Gran.

"Sorry you had to see that on the porch tonight, Dylan," Gran said, then winked at me.

"No, you're not," I told her.

"You're right," she said. She and Buddy started laughing. "We're headed over to the party at Rocky's Roadhouse. Care to join us?"

I frowned. "Seriously? You want my friends and me to go with you and Buddy to a bar?"

"Why not?" Buddy said. "You guys helped crack the case. Let me buy you a root beer."

"I think it's a cool idea, Gran," Monica said, and she hugged my grand-mother's arm.

"Sure is nice to have you back," Gran said "By the way, Buddy, this is Monica Buckley, the quick-witted young lady who saved your life."

Buddy's face broke into a wide grin. "I can't even tell you how glad I am to meet you," he said, then wrapped her in a huge bear hug. Monica looked shy as she hugged him back. I made a mental note to sign up soon for that first-aid course at the rec center.

Then Monica had her cell phone in her hand. "I'm calling Ivy Adams. Gonna tell her to meet us at Rocky's," she said. I watched Cory's mouth drop open. "Yeah, she kind of likes you too, Cory. So don't blow this, okay?"

Cory looked at me and smirked. "Best. Halloween. Ever," he said.

The bar was decorated like a haunted house. And packed, of course. All the adults in town seemed to be there in the most insane costumes. We said a quick hi to Mom and Brent, then grabbed a free table. I was starving and ordered a huge plate of wings and sweet-potato fries for Monica and me to share.

Ivy and Cory seemed to be getting along well, their heads together over a plate of nachos.

"So if you combine their names like Brangelina, they'd be called Ivory. Cool, huh?" Monica whispered.

"Only a girl would come up with that. I guess that makes us Dylica then," I said. "Hmm. Too bad my name isn't Harry."

After a quick pause, she gave me a wide smile. "Har*monica*! Hah, good one, Harry!"

We both started laughing like nut jobs, we were so giddy by then.

A few minutes later, I saw Nicole talking on her cell phone. I watched her face as she walked toward the rest-rooms to finish her call in a quieter place. I waited, because I figured she was getting the news about Charlie. And, sure enough, her hand was on my shoulder a few minutes later.

"Dylan, can I speak to you for a second?" she said, looking solemn.

"I guess you heard the news," I said. She nodded slowly. I followed her through the crowd and blasting rock music to the hallway outside the restrooms.

"Charlie Wells confessed tonight," she told me. "The whole thing was his idea. He knows that his step-granddad is loaded. And because his dad is still so close to Buddy Dalton, Charlie thought their family might get an inheritance when Buddy dies."

My throat felt dry, and I swallowed hard. "He was trying to knock him off by *scaring* him to death? What a sicko. So what about Tim? Was his real grandson in on this stupid plot too?"

"Tim got dragged into it by Charlie," Nicole explained. "Then Charlie warned him to keep his mouth shut after he got busted by the footage from your camera.

So Tim let Rick Smith take the fall instead. He was *scared*. Donahue told me Tim cried the entire time when they brought him in for questioning tonight."

"That is totally unreal," I said, shaking my head. I couldn't imagine ever doing something so awful to Gran. Then Nicole put her hand on my shoulder.

"So take some pity on your friend Tim Dalton," she said. "He feels like crap right now."

"That jerk is so *not* my friend," I told her. "He's just a dopey nose-picking follower."

Nicole smirked at me. "I seem to recall that you were a follower not that long ago," she said, knocking me on the head with her knuckles. "And look at you now. Big-time film director."

Hmm. Sometimes my godmother Nicole could make a good point.

After all the Halloween insanity, and all the craziness and partying at Rocky's Roadhouse, which went on until the bar closed at 1:00 AM, I was too pumped to sleep when I got home.

So instead I wrote the opening and closing voice-overs for *Rise of the Zombie Scarecrows*. It was way easier to do knowing how the epic ending would play out. Especially since we had such awesome footage of Garret's scarecrow-vandal takedown. I still had to figure out who would do one of the parts though.

I'd already decided that I would read the closing lines of this movie, since the whole thing was my idea. I also had a pretty cool idea about who could read the opening voice-over. I only hoped she'd agree.

We planned to meet in the park on Sunday afternoon before the scarecrow contest winners were announced. I knew it would be packed with people, so I got there early and reserved our favorite park bench, overlooking the lake. We'd been kissing there a lot the last couple of months. And now almost all the leaves were gone from the trees.

The reporter and photographer from the *Bridgewood Weekly* caught up with me as I was crossing the park. They'd arrived early, too, for interviews and photos.

"Hey, Dylan!" the reporter called. "Nice of you to let Garrett make the Monday edition. He'll be on the front page tomorrow, you know!"

"Yeah, well, what can I say. Crazy things happen a lot in this town," I told her. "And not always to me."

"I got some great shots of your zombie march on the main drag last night," the photographer added, and he nudged me. "Make sure we get a chance to see your flick, okay?"

"Don't worry. I'll send you both an invitation to the screening," I said. "You need to keep track of my career."

Then, over their shoulders, I saw Monica crossing the park. She'd shown up early. The reporter followed my sight line.

"I see your partner in crime has arrived," he said. Then he nudged me again.

"We'd better leave these two alone," the reporter told him. Then she smiled at me. "Sometimes I so wish I was your age again, Dylan," she said as the two of them walked off.

I hugged Monica when she reached me, and she hugged me back hard. Then we sat down on our special park bench. I dug into my backpack, pulled out two copies of the voice-overs and handed her one.

"Cool!" she said. "You actually did finish it!"

"Of course. It was easy. You're looking at the next Spielberg, after all."

"Dylan," she said, laughing. "You are totally crazy. You know that, right?"

"Well, you like crazy artsy types, right? And apparently you're known as my partner in crime in this town. According to the *Bridgewood Weekly* anyway. How awesome is that?"

"*Absolutely* awesome." Monica Buckley grinned at me. Then she took the piece of paper from my hand. And we both read our parts out loud...

OPENING SCENE. Camera shots panning scarecrows all over town.

VOICE-OVER (Monica)
It started that Halloween night. And it was all because of the scare-crows. It wasn't all their fault though. Eventually, scientists blamed the pigs for the tainted

straw that some of the scarecrows were stuffed with. Who would have thought a pig virus could infect a nonhuman? But, like they say, truth is stranger than fiction.

CLOSING SCENE.

VOICE-OVER (Dylan)
We finished it that Halloween night. With those lighters in our hands. And that was how we kept them away forever. With candles lit all over town. In every single window. Every single night. In this town, we don't dare blow out our candles. Ever.

Camera pans to lit jack-o'-lantern in window, zooms through nose to candle flame.

That's a wrap.

Deb Loughead is a regular contributor to the Orca Currents series. Two of her other titles, *The Snowball Effect* and *Caught in the Act*, also feature Dylan and his pals.